United States Department of Agriculture

I0409054

Economic Research Service

www.ers.usda.gov

Access this report online:

www.ers.usda.gov/publications/err-economic-research-report/err182

Download the charts contained in this report:

- Go to the report's index page www.ers.usda.gov/publications/
  err-economic-research-report/err182
- Click on the bulleted item "Download err182.zip"
- Open the chart you want, then save it to your computer

Recommended citation format for this publication:

Toole, Andrew A. and Fred Kuchler. *Improving Health Through Nutrition Research: An Overview of the U.S. Nutrition Research System,* ERR-182, U.S. Department of Agriculture, Economic Research Service, January 2015.

United States Department of Agriculture

Economic Research Service

Economic Research Report Number 182

January 2015

Improving Health Through Nutrition Research: An Overview of the U.S. Nutrition Research System

Andrew A. Toole and Fred Kuchler

Abstract

This report explores the structure and function of the U.S. nutrition research system, with an emphasis on trends in Federal support. It describes how nutrition research is used, especially for nutrition education and communication, but also for regulation and food assistance. The report uses the Human Nutrition Research Information Management database maintained by the National Institutes of Health to analyze long-term trends. Federal investments in nutrition research grew from 1985 to 2009 in real terms, but the portfolio of research changed. Over time, the share of nutrition research support by the U.S. Department of Health and Human Services increased while support by the U.S. Department of Agriculture decreased. This shift changed how research topics were selected and funded within the Federal portfolio. More research is funded through competitive grants than through intramural or formula funding, and a broader set of academic institutions now participates in nutrition research.

Keywords: Federal research, research and development, public investment, nutrition information system, Human Nutrition Research Information Management (HNRIM), formula funding, competitive funding

Acknowledgments

The authors would like to thank reviewers Laurian Unnevehr with the International Food Policy Research Institute; Parke Wilde with Tufts University; Amber Jessup, Office of the Assistant Secretary for Planning and Evaluation, and James Krebs-Smith, Division of Nutrition Research Coordination, National Institutes of Health, both with the U.S. Department of Health and Human Services; and an anonymous reviewer. In addition, we would like to thank our colleagues Keith Fuglie, Jean Buzby, Tom Hertz, and James MacDonald at the USDA Economic Research Service, USDA for their helpful comments. We thank Dale Simms for his editorial work and Cynthia A. Ray for design and layout.

Contents

Summary iii

Introduction 1

Paths From Nutrition Research to Better Health 2

    Public Sector Communication of Best Practices 3

    Public Sector Regulations and Policies 5

    Private Sector Innovation 8

The U.S. Nutrition Research System: Nature and Structure 9

    Federal Support for Nutrition Research 10

    National Trends in Federal Support for Nutrition Research. 11

Federal Portfolio of Nutrition Research Areas and Research Performers 15

    Defining Portfolio Shares Using HNRIM 15

    Distribution of Federal Support Across Major Nutrition Research Areas Is Relatively Stable . . 17

    Share of Support for *Disease, Injury,* and *Conditions* Research Increased Due to the
Obesity, Genetics, and *Other Diseases* Topic Areas 18

    Share of Support for *Metabolism and Metabolic Mechanisms* Research Decreased Due
to the *Vitamins, Minerals, and Proteins* Topic Areas 19

    Share of Support for *Food Sciences* Decreased Due to the
Food Composition and Effects of Technology on Foods and Diets Topic Areas 19

    The Portfolio of Federally Supported Organizations That Perform Nutrition Research 20

Conclusion 22

References 23

Appendix—The Relationship Between Project Counts and Project Awards 26

United States Department of Agriculture

Find the full report
at *www.ers.usda.
gov/publications/err-
economic-research-
report/err182*

Improving Health Through Nutrition Research: An Overview of the U.S. Nutrition Research System

Andrew A. Toole and Fred Kuchler

What Is the Issue?

A 2013 survey of consumers found that 45 percent were "very interested" and another 42 percent were "somewhat interested" in learning more about foods that have health benefits. Private companies are responding by redirecting their research and development efforts toward creating nutritionally enriched conventional foods and new food products that go beyond basic nutrition. Governmental organizations use programs and policies to address a variety of public health challenges such as malnutrition and obesity. The United States has a diverse and multi-disciplinary nutrition research system with numerous sponsoring organizations and thousands of active researchers. The body of knowledge this system produces serves as the foundation for progress toward better health. However, maintaining this foundation is not guaranteed; it depends on the resources provided by sponsoring organizations and on how research topics are selected and funded. This report explores the structure and function of the U.S. nutrition research system, with a particular emphasis on changes in Federal support.

What Did the Study Find?

Public data on the levels and trends in research investments are limited, particularly for private research organizations. However, data are available on federally supported nutrition research from the Human Nutrition Research Information Management (HNRIM) database maintained by the National Institutes of Health. Analysis of the HNRIM database for the 25 years from 1985 through 2009 (the latest year of available USDA data) revealed that Federal investments in nutrition research more than doubled in real terms, but the portfolio of research changed. The share of Federal support by the U.S. Department of Health and Human Services (DHHS) increased while that by the U.S. Department of Agriculture (USDA) decreased. This shift changed how research topics were selected and funded within the Federal portfolio. As a result, more research is funded through competitive grants than through intramural or formula funding, and a broader set of academic institutions now participates in nutrition research.

To analyze the nutrition research areas receiving Federal support, we construct a portfolio that shows the shares (percent of all nutrition research projects) across 6 major research areas spanning 37 topics. The analysis finds:

- The *Disease, Injury, and Conditions* research area grew most in its share of Federal support, climbing from 40 percent in 1985 to 49 percent by 2009. This area covers a wide

ERS is a primary source of economic research and analysis from the U.S. Department of Agriculture, providing timely informa-tion on economic and policy issues related to agriculture, food, the environment, and rural America.

www.ers.usda.gov

range of diseases (e.g., cardiovascular, diabetes, and cancer) and conditions (e.g., obesity, anorexia, and high cholesterol).

- Within the Disease, Injury, and Conditions research area, the *Obesity/Anorexia/Appetite Control* topic grew fastest, rising from 3.6 percent of the Federal portfolio in 1985 to 13.1 percent in 2009. This topic area grew fastest within the portfolios of both DHHS and USDA.

- The *Metabolism and Metabolic Mechanisms* research area experienced the largest decline in Federal portfolio share, from 28 percent in 1985 to 20 percent in 2009. This area investigates how the human body gets or makes energy from food and its constituents such as carbohydrates and proteins.

- Seven out of the nine topic areas that make up the *Metabolism and Metabolic Mechanisms* research area experienced declining Federal shares between 1985 and 2009. The topics leading this decline were *Vitamins, Minerals, and Proteins.*

- The USDA provides most of the Federal support for nutrition research in the *Food Sciences* area, which includes food processing, preservation, and other food-related technologies. From 1985 to 2009, USDA supported 80 percent of the active projects (on average).

- The Federal portfolio share allocated to *Food Sciences* decreased from 10 to 4 percent in the period analyzed. While the Federal shares for each of the four topic areas within the *Food Sciences* fell, the topics leading the decline were *Food Composition* and *Effects of Technology on Foods and Diets.*

The portfolio of federally supported organizations that perform nutrition research also shifted from 1985 to 2009:

- The share of Federal nutrition research projects performed by *Government researchers* fell from 12 percent in 1985 to 6 percent in 2009.

- The share of research projects performed by *land-grant universities and colleges* fell from 34 percent in 1985 to 22 percent in 2009.

- The share of research performed by *non-land grant universities and colleges* grew from 30 percent in 1985 to 41 percent of total nutrition projects in 2009.

- The *Other* category of institutions—*medical schools, hospitals, and research institutes*—also saw its share of research support grow, from 22 percent to 29 percent of all federally supported nutrition projects.

- *Private companies* performed just 1-2 percent of federally supported nutrition research projects.

Our review of the academic and policy literatures found no published studies that analyzed the impacts of these trends on the volume of research performed or the productivity of the U.S. nutrition research system. Future studies could analyze available indicators of research outputs, such as published articles or patents, and could relate those to inputs, such as project effort or financial investments.

How Was the Study Conducted?

This report synthesizes the existing literature analyzing the U.S. nutrition research system and analyzes data on Federal support from the Human Nutrition Research Information Management (HNRIM) database. This database is maintained by the National Institutes of Health (NIH) under the auspices of the Interagency Committee on Human Nutrition Research. Each participating Federal agency reports to HNRIM its own data on active nutrition projects each year. To document the nature and trends in Federal nutrition research, this report relies on the number and distribution of active project counts contained in HNRIM for fiscal years 1985 through 2009. Based on an analysis of available data on project award amounts, we concluded that project counts accurately characterize trends in Federal support for nutrition research.

Improving Health Through Nutrition Research: An Overview of the U.S. Nutrition Research System

Introduction

U.S. consumers, private companies, and governmental organizations are all keenly interested in the relationships between nutrition, dietary choices, and health. In 2013, a survey by the International Food Information Council found that 45 percent of consumers were "very interested" and another 42 percent were "somewhat interested" in learning more about foods that have health benefits (IFIC, 2013). Private companies are responding to consumers by redirecting their research and development efforts toward creating nutritionally enriched conventional foods and new food products that go beyond basic nutrition. Governmental organizations use programs and policies to address a variety of public health challenges such as malnutrition and obesity.

The links between nutrition, dietary choices, and health are established through research. *Basic research* reveals the genetic, cellular, and chemical relationships that determine metabolic responses to diet and food components. For instance, *nutrigenetics/nutrigenomics research* is expected to produce new nutritional and disease biomarkers based on how nutrients interact with genes, proteins, and metabolites for specific individuals (Ohlhorst et al., 2013). *Clinical research* translates basic research into evidence-based policy and practice. These studies are critical for demonstrating nutrient dosages, absorption, efficacy, and safety for health interventions. *Observational research* focuses on a variety of topics including nutritional epidemiology, nutrition education, and program evaluations. Insights into food consumption habits and behaviors from these studies help to improve food choices, policies, and regulations.

As a whole, this body of nutrition research underpins progress toward better health. However, maintaining and strengthening this knowledge foundation depends on resources provided by sponsoring organizations and on how research topics are selected and funded. For instance, changes in Federal budget appropriations across agencies affect not only the level of Federal support but also how Federal support is administered. When Federal agencies have different missions, use different funding mechanisms, and support different performers within the nutrition research system, these funding changes may alter the nature of nutrition research by favoring some topics and performers over others or affecting research productivity. This report provides a first look at the structure and function of the U.S. nutrition research system, with an emphasis on changes in Federal support.

Improving Health Through Nutrition Research: An Overview of the U.S. Nutrition Research System, ERR-182
Economic Research Service/USDA

Paths From Nutrition Research to Better Health

Nutrition research produces information that influences human health through a variety of paths within a complex communication system, composed of information generation, translation, and impact (fig. 1). Information generation, carried out by the nutrition research system, is the stage where researchers discover new knowledge, methods, and technologies. For example, in 2007, researchers identified the so-called "fat mass and obesity-associated" (FTO) gene variant, which is present in about one out of every six adults in the population. People with the FTO gene variant have a 20- to 30-percent higher risk of obesity compared to those without the variant (Harvard School of Public Health, 2014). Other researchers are using this information to understand how the FTO gene variant triggers weight gain. In a 2013 study, Rachel Batterham and her research team identified another link. She described it as follows:

> We've known for a while that variations in the FTO gene are strongly linked with obesity, but until now we didn't know why. What this study shows us is that individuals with two copies of the obesity-risk FTO variant are biologically programmed to eat more. Not only do these people have higher ghrelin levels and therefore feel hungrier, their brains respond differently to ghrelin and to pictures of food—it's a double hit. (University College London, 2013)

Discoveries like the FTO gene variant are communicated through a variety of channels, such as publications, conferences, interpersonal networks, and consulting, to the next component—information translation. Information translation is essential because consumers rarely draw information directly from the scientific journals or other communication channels used by nutrition researchers. Instead, consumers rely on various public and private organizations to evaluate, interpret, and repackage nutrition research findings to facilitate understanding and guide behaviors. These translational activities include public-sector communication of best practices, public-sector regulations and policies, and private-sector products and services (fig. 1). The connection between nutrition research and each of these translational activities is discussed below in separate subsections.

The findings from nutrition research need to be accessible and understandable before consumers can use this information to improve their choices about food and diet. Consumer choices, in turn, influence short-term and long-term health. For instance, dietary choices affect the extent and severity of diseases such as cardiovascular disease and conditions such as anemia, anorexia, and obesity. The trends and costs associated with nutrition-related diseases and conditions are significant concerns within the public health community. Obesity rates among adults increased by 37 percent between 1998 and 2006, with an obese adult spending $1,429 more on health care than a normal-weight person in 2006 (Finkelstein et al., 2009). And these obesity-driven increases in health care costs are likely to continue. After a review of recent epidemiological studies, the Centers for Disease Control and Prevention (CDC) concluded that "children and adolescents who are obese are likely to be obese as adults" and "childhood obesity has more than doubled in children and quadrupled in adolescents in the past 30 years" (CDC, 2014).

The value of nutrition research ultimately derives from its potential impact on human health. While the health effects of the research described in this report have not been quantified, it is clear that even a small impact on health would produce very large economic benefits. Two economists at the University of Chicago, Kevin Murphy and Robert Topel, developed a framework for understanding the economic value created by better health. Their framework considered two aspects of health improvements—life expectancy and health status. Improved life expectancy allows people to enjoy

Figure 1
Schematic of the nutrition information communication system

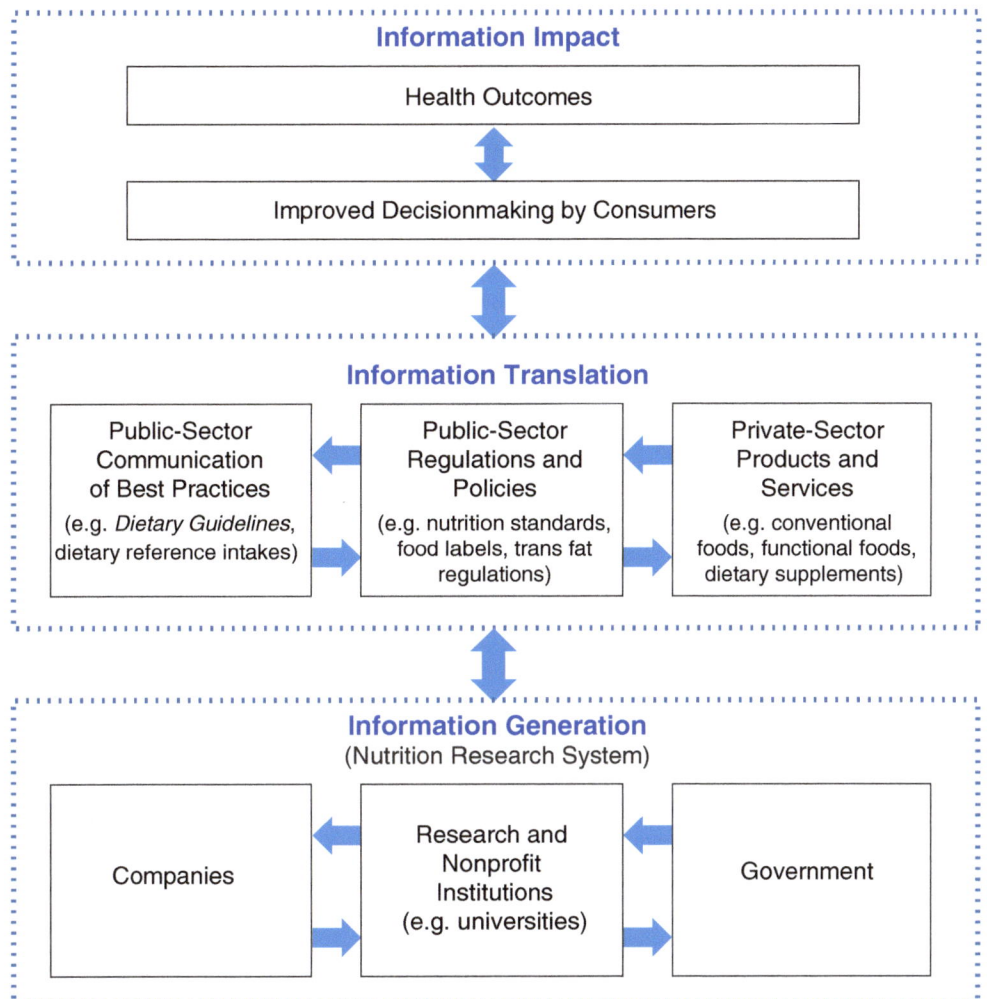

Source: USDA, Economic Research Service, author's calculations.

more products, services, and leisure activities over their lifetime. Improved health status means people have a higher quality of life (e.g., better eyesight or better mobility), and this allows them to more fully enjoy life. Murphy and Topel (2006) estimated the economic value of improved life expectancy that occurred in the United States between 1970 and 2000 at $95 trillion, or about $3.2 trillion per year (see box on the "Murphy and Topel Estimates").

Public-Sector Communication of Best Practices

The *Dietary Guidelines for Americans* exemplifies how the public sector communicates best practices based on nutrition research. Since 1980, the U.S. Department of Health and Human Services (DHHS) and the U.S. Department of Agriculture (USDA) have worked together to develop and disseminate the *Dietary Guidelines for Americans*.[1] The *Guidelines*, released every 5 years, provide recommendations for a nutritionally balanced diet developed from a review of relevant scientific evidence.

---

[1]The 1995 *Dietary Guidelines* was the first mandated joint report, prepared according to the 1990 National Nutrition Monitoring and Related Research Act. Among the requirements, reports are reviewed by a committee of experts, updated if necessary, and published every 5 years.

Murphy and Topel Estimates: Perspective and Approach to Health Valuation

The $95-trillion economic gain calculated by Murphy and Topel is enormous. To put this in perspective, Murphy and Topel compared their figure with the gross domestic product (GDP) of the United States. The U.S. GDP measures the market value of all final goods and services produced by labor and property located in the United States. Economists and policymakers use the GDP to assess the levels and trends in U.S. output and economic growth. Similarly, Murphy and Topel view annual health improvements as health "output" that adds to the well-being of Americans. Making this comparison, the $95 trillion Murphy and Topel calculated from increased life expectancy over 1970 to 2000 is equivalent to 44 percent of the cumulative GDP for the United States over the same period. In other words, the value afforded Americans through improved life expectancy was equal to 44 percent of the total value of all final goods and services produced in the United States over those years.

Why are the estimated values for health improvements so large? As Murphy and Topel point out, the economic gains are large because the number of people who benefit from the health improvements is large. Murphy and Topel started with the observation that during the 20th century, life expectancy at birth for a typical American increased by 30 years. The value of greater longevity and better health, however, is not like the value of cars, toasters, or other things that might be purchased in retail stores at a known price. Instead, the value of greater longevity and better health must be estimated indirectly. Murphy and Topel based their valuation on how much a person would pay (called "willingness to pay") for a risk reduction, where the risks considered influence the length and quality of the person's life.

Of course, measuring the value of risk reduction is not easy compared to measuring the value of other product attributes that are priced in the market. For example, Coca-Cola soft drinks are usually more expensive than generic colas of the same size. This price premium for Coca-Cola indicates the value consumers place on the Coca-Cola brand. Product labels make it easy for consumers to compare prices and many product attributes, but few products indicate the degree of riskiness. For instance, no one sells chicken parts with labels indicating the likelihood of contracting a *Salmonella* infection. Peoples' willingness to pay for risk reduction, however, can be detected in some market transactions, and economists use those transactions to estimate the value of risk reductions. The standard approach is to look at job market transactions, although product market transactions (e.g., purchases of bicycle helmets) and housing market transactions (e.g., home purchases in locations at risk for a hazardous waste site) are also used in some studies. In the job market, people are generally paid more to perform riskier jobs, and economists have estimated how much wages rise when workers accept a small risk of on-the-job fatal injury using information from jobs in mining, construction, manufacturing, and many other industries (Viscusi and Aldy, 2003). From this, economists estimate the risk-dollar tradeoffs individuals are willing to accept.

Murphy and Topel used risk-dollar tradeoffs from job market studies to estimate a yearly value of a "statistical life" at every age. They benchmarked their analysis to studies estimating that workers demand a $630 annual wage premium to accept a 1-in-10,000 risk of fatal injury. That is, across 10,000 workers accepting the wage premium and the risk, we expect to see one fatal injury for an increased wage bill of $6.3 million. In their analysis, $6.3 million is the average value of a statistical life for working-age adults, a figure obtained from the U.S. Environmental Protection Agency. Based on this, Murphy and Topel created an annual version called the "value of a life-year" for an individual at every age, beginning at birth and extending to death as determined by the mortality tables for the United States.

Using the observed increase in life expectancy in the United States, Murphy and Topel calculated the increase in the value of a life-year for an individual. Then, for individuals at each age, they summed the increased life-year values over the remaining years in the person's lifespan. This produces a total increase (or gain) in the value of

continued—

an individual's statistical life at each age. They still have two more steps in their calculation. First, to calculate the economic value across all people in an age group, they must multiply the increased value of life at each age by the population in that age group. They do this for the current population and for future populations as future generations are also expected to benefit from increased life expectancy. This step dramatically increases their estimated gains because there are millions of people in the population at each age. Now, with the total benefits for each age group, the final economic value is reached by summing across all the age groups in the current population as well as those expected to benefit in future populations.

The science-based process of creating the *Guidelines* begins with the selection of an independent Dietary Guidelines Advisory Committee (DGAC) composed of nationally recognized experts in the fields of nutrition and health. These individuals are responsible for making recommendations to the Secretaries of DHHS and USDA after a thorough review of current scientific and medical knowledge. The DGAC uses the Nutrition Evidence Library (NEL) to support its systematic review. The NEL reviews, evaluates, synthesizes and houses the information produced by the nutrition research system and posts full "evidence portfolios" online (see http://www.nel.gov/).

The *Guidelines* are the foundation for educational materials like *MyPlate* distributed by the USDA and other Federal agencies. By law,[2] all Federal dietary guidance for the public—including print and Web-based educational materials, messages, tools, and programs to communicate healthy eating and physical activity information—must be consistent with the *Guidelines*.

But the influence of the *Guidelines* does not end with advice. The *Guidelines* influence the level and type of food assistance offered through the 15 food and nutrition assistance programs administered by USDA's Food and Nutrition Service. USDA's Center for Nutrition Policy and Promotion relies on the *Guidelines* as the nutritional basis for its *USDA Food Plans* (Thrifty, Low-Cost, Moderate-Cost, and Liberal). The Thrifty Food Plan is an estimate of how much it costs to buy food and to prepare nutritious, low-cost meals for a household. That estimate is periodically revised for consistency with the *Guidelines* and is the basis for household allotments under the Supplemental Nutrition Assistance Program (SNAP–formerly the Food Stamp Program). The *Guidelines* are an input into determining food benefits under the Special Supplemental Nutrition Program for Women, Infants, and Children (WIC).[3] And the *Guidelines* influence meal standards for the National School Lunch Program.

Public-Sector Regulations and Policies

Nutrition research is also an integral source of information for regulations and policies such as the Federal regulations on retail food labels. Under the Nutrition Labeling and Education Act (NLEA) of 1990, the U.S. Food and Drug Administration (FDA) establishes how food manufacturers will account for nutrients in foods—the Nutrition Facts panel on processed foods—and modifies those standards periodically (see box, "Trans Fats Labeling"). Another example is USDA's nutrition standards for all foods sold in schools, including snacks and vending machine foods that compete with federally supported meals programs. The Healthy, Hunger-Free Kids Act of 2010 requires USDA to establish nutrition standards for all foods sold in schools—beyond the federally supported meals programs. The *Smart Snacks in School* nutrition standards drew on recommendations from the Institute of Medicine and voluntary standards already implemented by schools around the country (FNS, 2013).

---

[2]National Nutrition Monitoring and Related Research Act.

[3]There are other inputs into determining food benefits for WIC as the *Guidelines* do not cover children under age 2, a major part of the WIC caseload.

Nutrition Research Supports Federal Food Labeling Regulations— *Trans Fats Labeling*

While the use of trans fats in food manufacturing became widespread in the 1940s (DHHS, FDA, 2013), their use is now declining (Rahkovsky et al., 2012). Trans fats were commonly used in food processing because hydrogenation allowed food processors to raise the melting point of relatively inexpensive products containing polyunsaturated fatty acids, making the products solid at room temperature.[1] Foods that are higher in saturated fatty acids are more resistant to spoilage. The twin attractions of these synthetic trans fatty acids, found in partially hydrogenated oils, are reduced costs of food production and longer shelf life of products. Partially hydrogenated oils have frequently been used in margarines, snack foods, and prepared desserts, replacing saturated fatty acids.

Trans fats made it easier for food manufacturers to develop tasty snacks, and their snacks cost less to make than if they had used other saturated fats. Consumers likely shared in those benefits as the cost reductions kept retail prices of snack foods down. However, nutrition research identified a downside to the widespread use of trans fats in manufactured foods, as summarized by the Institute of Medicine (part of the National Academy of Sciences):

> *Trans fatty acids are not essential and provide no known benefit to human health. Therefore, no AI or RDA is set. As with saturated fatty acids, there is a positive linear trend between trans fatty acid intake and LDL cholesterol concentration, and therefore increased risk of CHD. A UL is not set for trans fatty acids because any incremental increase in trans fatty acid intake increases CHD risk.[2]*

The Federal Government has pursued two activities intended to reduce Americans' dietary intake of trans fats:

1. Informing consumers that they can reduce health risks by choosing fats other than trans fats, and

2. Requiring food manufacturers to label the trans fats content of foods.

Informing consumers

The recommendation to minimize intake of trans fats began with the *Dietary Guidelines for Americans, 2005*.[3]

> *Consume less than 10 percent of calories from saturated fatty acids and less than 300 mg/day of cholesterol, and keep trans fatty acid consumption as low as possible.*

At that time, the Food Guide Pyramid emphasized the benefits of reducing foods high in trans fatty acids.

The 2010 *Dietary Guidelines* offers additional advice on how to minimize trans fat consumption:

> *Keep trans fatty acid consumption as low as possible, especially by limiting foods that contain synthetic sources of trans fats, such as partially hydrogenated oils, and by limiting other solid fats.*

---

[1] *Dietary Guidelines for Americans*, 2010, Part D Section 3: Fatty Acids and Cholesterol, p. D3-7.

[2] AI, Adequate Intake, is defined as the recommended average daily intake level. RDA, Recommended Dietary Allowance, is defined as the average daily dietary nutrient intake level sufficient to meet nutrient requirements. UL, Tolerable Upper Intake Level, is defined as the highest average daily nutrient intake level that is likely to pose no risk of adverse health effects to almost all individuals in the general population. Coronary heart disease is abbreviated as CHD.

[3] Because trans fatty acids are unavoidable in ordinary, nonvegan diets, consuming 0 percent of them as energy would require significant changes in patterns of dietary intake. As with saturated fatty acids, such adjustments may introduce undesirable effects (e.g., elimination of commercially prepared foods, dairy products, and meats that contain trans fatty acids may result in inadequate intakes of protein and certain micronutrients) and unknown and unquantifiable health risks. Nevertheless, it is recommended that trans fatty acid consumption be as low as possible while consuming a nutritionally adequate diet. (Institute of Medicine, 2005, pp. 423-24)

continued—

In November 1999, the U.S. Food and Drug Administration (FDA) proposed a rule that would require the amount of trans fatty acids present in foods to be included in the product's Nutrition Facts panel. In 2003, the rule became final with requirements for labeling beginning in 2006.

In its November 1999 proposed rule, FDA described the nutrition research studies that it relied on. It had to establish that dietary intake of trans fats could be linked to adverse health outcomes—increases in LDL-C would imply a consequent increase in rates of coronary heart disease (CHD). FDA also had to gauge the magnitude of the problem, showing how much trans fats Americans were consuming. And it had to quantify how different types of Government intervention would improve health outcomes. FDA relied on studies published between 1988 and 1995 (p. 41442 in final rule). The most problematic studies were those examining the linkage between dietary intake of trans fats and CHD. These included controlled intervention studies, which tested for a causal relationship between trans fat consumption and CHD, and epidemiological studies, which established associations between trans fat consumption and CHD. FDA interpreted the results from published studies as "evolving." Some studies pointed to trans fats raising LDL-C levels (the primary risk factor for CHD) as much as cholesterol-raising saturated fatty acids, while others found no adverse effect. Between the November 1999 proposal and the July 2003 final rule, additional studies reinforced FDA's conclusion that trans fat consumption raised LDL-C levels and increased CHD risk.

FDA's estimates of the intake of trans fats were established by drawing on several sources, but largely came from USDA's Continuing Survey of Food Intakes by Individuals and from USDA-ERS figures on fats and oils production and food disappearance data (recognized as an overestimate).

FDA relied on its own survey of consumer behavior to gauge how much consumers might respond to finding trans fats on nutrition facts panels. While many studies link diet and health outcomes, behavioral studies of label use relevant to trans fats are still few.

In November 2013, FDA announced that additional scientific evidence led the agency to tentatively determine that partially hydrogenated oils—the primary source of trans fats in manufactured foods—are not generally recognized as safe for any use in food. If the tentative determination is supported, partially hydrogenated oils would be considered food additives and their use in food manufacturing subject to regulation.

Driving the tentative determination were new research findings. FDA's own studies pointed to trans fat consumption trending lower as foods were reformulated. However, new studies of health risks pointed to increased risk of CHD from any amount of trans fat. Other new studies found, with varying degrees of certainty, that trans fat consumption may worsen insulin resistance or raise diabetes risk. Clearly, as research results unfold, the regulatory process responds.

> Food policies, like requirements for iodine fortification in salt or the enrichment of flour products with B vitamins and iron, eliminated many nutritional deficiencies in the United States (Davis and Saltos, 1999). For instance, iodine deficiency impedes the proper functioning of the thyroid and is associated with a number of disorders including brain damage in children. In 1996, the FDA established regulations requiring that by 1998 all standardized enriched cereal grain products sold in the United States include 140 micrograms of folic acid per 100 grams, and allowed for the addition of folic acid to breakfast cereals, corn grits, infant formulas, medical foods, and foods for special dietary use. Before fortification, about 4,130 U.S. babies had neural tube defects each year and nearly

1,200 died. After folic acid fortification, the yearly number of pregnancies affected by neural tube defects dropped to about 3,000, and related deaths declined to 840 (CDC, 2004).

The notion that the Federal Government might solve or at least mitigate specific health problems by requiring the addition of micronutrients could only come from research demonstrating that such micronutrients are critical to avoiding a disease. However, a single research finding is unlikely to justify new regulations. Federal rulemaking and regulations are predicated on results from across the spectrum of nutrition research. Studies on nutrient metabolism, dietary intake, food consumption habits, and the effect of regulations on food choices are all critical links in demonstrating whether Federal intervention in dietary issues is worthwhile.

Private-Sector Innovation

As consumers demand healthier food and beverage products, the need for nutrition research to underscore these innovative products has grown. One approach to product innovation focuses on reformulating conventional food products to increase or decrease particular nutrients such as fat, sodium, and fiber. Companies can market these changes to consumers by using health- and nutrition-related claims, which are regulated by the FDA under the Nutrition Labeling and Education Act of 1990. In 2009, sales of products with sodium-, fat-, and calorie-related claims reached $73 billion (Martinez, 2013).

Another approach to product innovation, called "functional foods," is based on the idea that foods and drinks can provide health benefits beyond basic nutrition. No legal definition exists for functional foods in the United States, and the FDA regulates this type of food according to its classification as conventional food (e.g., garlic, nuts, and tomatoes), modified food (e.g., fortified, enriched, or enhanced), a food additive, a dietary supplement, a medical food, or a food for special dietary use (Academy of Nutrition and Dietetics, 2009). Functional foods are one of the fastest growing product categories in the food and beverage industries. According to Price Waterhouse Coopers (2009), U.S. revenues in the functional foods segment are growing at an average annual rate between 8.5 and 20 percent, whereas overall (food) industry revenue growth is at 1 to 4 percent.

The health connection that qualifies particular foods and beverages as functional foods is established through nutrition research. The Institute for Food Technologists outlined a process for bringing functional foods to market, whereby the nutrition research system (1) identifies the relationship between a food component and a health outcome, (2) demonstrates efficacy and intake levels, and (3) determines safety at efficacious levels (IFT, 2005). For instance, phytosterols are essential components of plant membranes that occur naturally in a variety of foods such as vegetables, fruits, and legumes. Nutrition research has shown that daily consumption of 2-3 grams will reduce serum LDL cholesterol and thus lower the risk of coronary heart disease (Demonty et al., 2009). Phytosterols are now added to many foods and beverages such as orange juice, cereals, yogurts, and granola bars.

The U.S. Nutrition Research System: Nature and Structure

The nutrition research system is foundational in that it generates the new knowledge and technologies that fuel improvements in food, dietary choices, and health outcomes. As such, continuing scientific progress toward understanding the relationships between human nutrition and health depends on maintaining a productive nutrition research system. This section describes the nature of nutrition research, the institutions that support nutrition research, available data, and trends in Federal support.

The field of human nutrition research is diverse and multidisciplinary. In 1980, the Joint Subcommittee on Human Nutrition Research formed by the Office of Science and Technology Policy defined nutrition research as those studies producing "new knowledge to improve the understanding of nutrition as it relates to human health and disease" (GAO, 1982). This definition includes disciplines such as food and plant sciences, biomedicine, behavioral science, education, communication, and economics. It cuts across the full research spectrum from basic science to health policy and from discovery to application.

The support for nutrition research activities comes from a variety of sources. In the private sector, profits motivate companies to innovate, undertake in-house research and development (R&D), and sponsor research in universities and government labs. Data on U.S. private R&D investments into nutrition research are not publicly available. However, private sector nutrition research is part of total R&D investments in the food and beverage industries, and we can gauge these latter investments. In 2007, Statistics Canada conducted a representative survey of Canadian companies active in the functional foods and natural health products markets (i.e., dietary supplements), which are the nutrition research-intensive market segments in the food and beverage industries. The survey indicated that 68 percent of the firms in the functional foods segment and 48 percent in the natural health products segment were engaged in R&D and spent a total of 148 million Canadian dollars in 2007 (Cinnamon, 2009). USDA's Economic Research Service estimated total R&D investments by the food and beverage industry at over $3.2 billion in 2006 (Fuglie et al., 2011). Even a small fraction of this total devoted to nutrition research would represent a substantial private-sector commitment.

Universities and other nonprofit organizations also support U.S. nutrition research. Here again, publicly available data are limited so it is difficult to draw precise inferences about relative magnitudes of financial support. The National Science Foundation's Higher Education R&D Survey is the main source for information on R&D conducted at U.S. universities and colleges. A breakout by academic discipline is not available, but the survey data are broken out according to the type of funding source. From 2001 to 2011, higher education institutions funded an average of 19 percent of total university- and college-performed R&D, and other nonprofit sources such as foundations funded an average of 7 percent (NSF, 2013). As human nutrition research is likely to be only a small fraction of total university R&D, the level of support provided by research and nonprofit organizations appears to be small relative to industry and government sources.

Federal and State governments appear to be the largest supporters of U.S. nutrition research, which makes sense from an economics perspective. Nutrition research produces new knowledge that economists associate with "public goods." With public goods, the incentives driving private companies to invest are small even when the benefits that consumers enjoy are large (Ribaudo et al., 2008). The problem is that private companies may not be able to earn enough profits from the products, services, and technologies that flow from their nutrition research investments to make

Improving Health Through Nutrition Research: An Overview of the U.S. Nutrition Research System, ERR-182
Economic Research Service/USDA

such investments worth undertaking. For example, the genetic research that led to the identification of the "obesity gene" was not immediately or eminently marketable. Public support can offset this problem by funding research in areas where private companies are unwilling to invest (or invest very little) due to insufficient incentives.

Federal Support for Nutrition Research

Systematic data on Federal support for nutrition research and training are available from the Human Nutrition Research Information Management (HNRIM) system.[4] This database is maintained by the National Institutes of Health (NIH). Each participating Federal agency provides its own data on active nutrition projects each year to form the HNRIM database. Since 1985, when the HNRIM database became operational, participating agencies have included the U.S. Department of Health and Human Services (DHHS), the U.S. Department of Agriculture (USDA), and six other Federal agencies (the Department of Veteran Affairs, the Agency for International Development, the U.S. Department of Defense, the U.S. Department of Commerce, the National Science Foundation, and the National Aeronautics and Space Administration).

The HNRIM database includes records for active nutrition research and training projects in each fiscal year. A multiyear project has multiple records in the database, one for every year the project is active. Across time, new projects enter the database, and completed projects are no longer reported to the database. This change in the number of active projects is used to characterize the evolution of Federal support for nutrition research for fiscal years 1985 through 2009.[5] Over that 25-year period, HNRIM contains 100,405 project records.[6] Project records in HNRIM also include a nutrition percentage (from 1 to 100) that adjusts for the relevance of the project to the field of nutrition. When each annual project is scaled by its nutrition relevance, the total number of federally supported nutrition research projects in HNRIM for fiscal years 1985 through 2009 is 67,958. In this analysis, all project statistics are calculated and reported accounting for the nutrition percentages.

To document the nature of and trends in nutrition research and training, our analysis uses the number and distribution of active project counts contained in HNRIM.[7] Based on analysis of available data on project award amounts, we concluded that project counts better characterize Federal research trends (see the appendix for more details). Overall, the HNRIM data on financial awards are not comprehensive enough to perform a comparative analysis.

Other than DHHS, all Federal agencies that support nutrition research reported $0 as the financial support for a significant number of projects. For USDA projects, 15 percent show $0 as the funding amount. For the six remaining agencies, about 63 percent of the projects report $0 as the funding amount. It is possible for a project to be completed after its planned end date, and some projects operate for a time through no-cost extensions. Reporting $0 would be appropriate for no-cost extensions, but it is also possible that the financial data for these projects are missing from HNRIM.

---

[4]We could not find any data sources that report human nutrition research by State governments.

[5]In this report all data are presented in fiscal years (FY) and are referred to simply as years. The most recent data reported are for FY 2009 (October 1, 2008 – September 30, 2009). The method for assigning projects to the field of nutrition and its subfields (or topic areas) changed in ways that make it impossible to compare pre- and post-2009 data.

[6]Throughout this report, the annual number of active project records is simply referred to as projects, even though these may be ongoing components of broader multiyear research efforts.

[7]This report does not count Federal support for company innovation or commercialization activities, facilities construction, or repair as part of research or training. Research and training projects are not analyzed separately and the combination is simply referred to as nutrition research.

10

Improving Health Through Nutrition Research: An Overview of the U.S. Nutrition Research System, ERR-182
Economic Research Service/USDA

Because no-cost extensions represent ongoing nutrition research and these projects cannot, with certainty, be distinguished from projects missing financial data, we present overall trends in Federal support using expenditures and project counts. When analyzing research area components, project counts are used.

National Trends in Federal Support for Nutrition Research

Over the last decade, the DHHS and USDA supported almost all Federal nutrition research projects. HNRIM data show that since 1998, the other 6 agencies reported 51 projects, or less than 0.2 percent of the total. In the mid-1990s, the other six agencies made up a more significant share. In 1993 and 1994, they accounted for 17 percent of active nutrition research projects, but by 2005 their share had dropped to zero. Although the HNRIM database does not show any active projects for the other six agencies after 2005, one cannot conclude that these agencies did not support any nutrition-related research. Participation in the HNRIM system is voluntary, and reporting may have stopped for other reasons. Nevertheless, as projects supported by agencies other than DHHS and USDA are a consistently small share of the total, for the remainder of this discussion we refer to the totals of DHHS and USDA as the Federal total, and our focus is on projects supported by DHHS and USDA.[8]

Federal financial investments into nutrition research more than doubled from 1985 to 2009, growing at an average annual rate of 3 percent (fig. 2). All of this growth is due to increased DHHS funding, especially between 1999 and 2003. In those 5 years, Congress implemented its plan to double the budget of the National Institutes of Health (NIH), which is the lead agency within DHHS supporting nutrition research. USDA funding fell at an average annual rate of 1.4 percent between 1985 and 2009.

When charted by active Federal nutrition projects, the overall Federal and agency-specific results are quite similar (fig. 3); however, the "kink" in the expenditures trend from the doubling of the NIH budget is no longer apparent. This suggests that increasing project size (i.e., dollars per project) absorbed a lot of the NIH budget increase. Nevertheless, the number of federally supported nutrition research projects more than doubled from 1985 to 2009, growing at an average annual rate of 2.9 percent. Nutrition projects numbered 2,178 in 1985 and 4,419 in 2009. This growth was the result of increasing support by DHHS and decreasing support by USDA. From 1999 to 2009, the number of DHHS-supported projects grew 7.4 percent annually while USDA-supported projects fell by 2.8 percent.

The aggregate trends in Federal support for nutrition research largely reflect budget appropriations to DHHS, particularly the NIH. As the NIH budget grew, the share allocated to nutrition research remained nearly constant and averaged about 4 percent per year from 1985 through 2009 (see HNRIM reports at http://hnrim.nih.gov/yearlyreports.aspx). For USDA, there may have been some reallocation of research effort. Since 1985, USDA public research expenditures remained nearly constant as the number of active nutrition research projects declined (http://www.ers.usda.gov/data-products/agricultural-research-funding-in-the-public-and-private-sectors.aspx). These trends tipped

---

[8]The Federal roles of the USDA and DHHS in human nutrition research were established in the National Agricultural Research, Extension, and Teaching Policy Act of 1977. That legislation directed the USDA to establish a separate and distinct mission to support research into food and human nutrition. It also designated the USDA as lead agency of the Federal Government for human nutrition research except for the biomedical aspects that relate to the diagnosis and treatment of disease, which were reserved for the U.S. Department of Health, Education, and Welfare (HEW), which later became DHHS. Prior to the passage of the Act, the Secretaries of HEW and USDA recognized their mutual interests in human nutrition research and signed an agreement for sharing their responsibilities (Rosenberg, 2009).

11

Improving Health Through Nutrition Research: An Overview of the U.S. Nutrition Research System, ERR-182
Economic Research Service/USDA

the balance of Federal support for nutrition research heavily toward DHHS. In the 25-year period covered by the data, the share of total Federal support provided by the USDA fell from 29 to 14 percent, on net, with a concurrent rise in the DHHS share to 86 percent by 2009.

Figure 2
Federal expenditures for nutrition research projects, 1985-2009

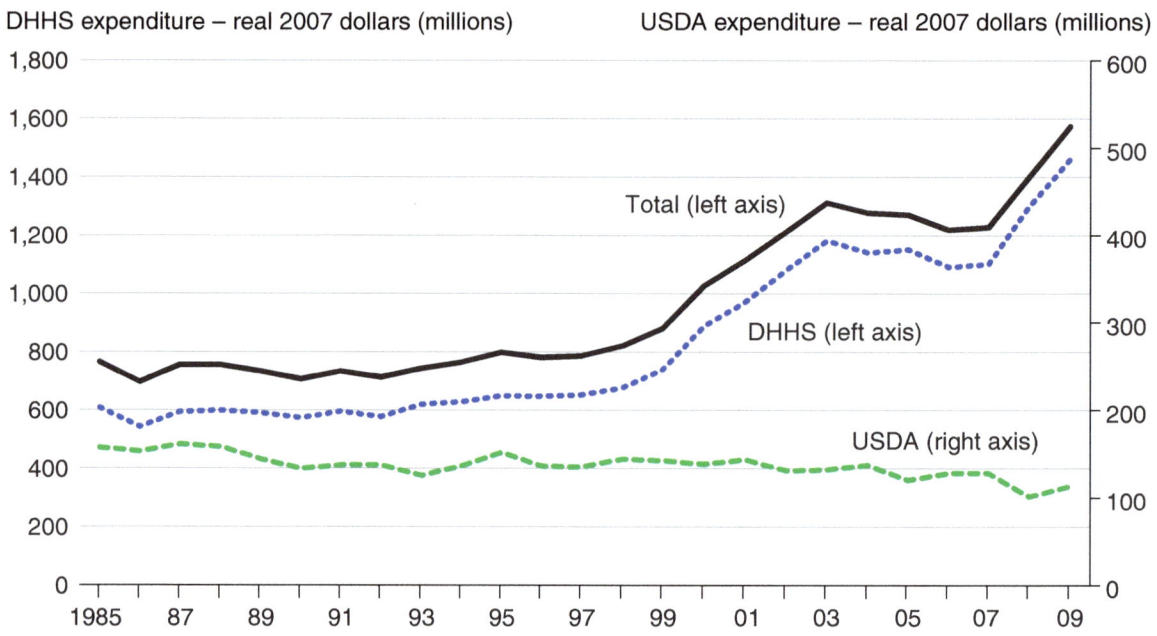

Source: USDA, Economic Research Service based on Human Nutrition Research Information Management data and the Biomedical Research and Development Price Index.

Figure 3
Federally supported nutrition research projects, 1985-2009

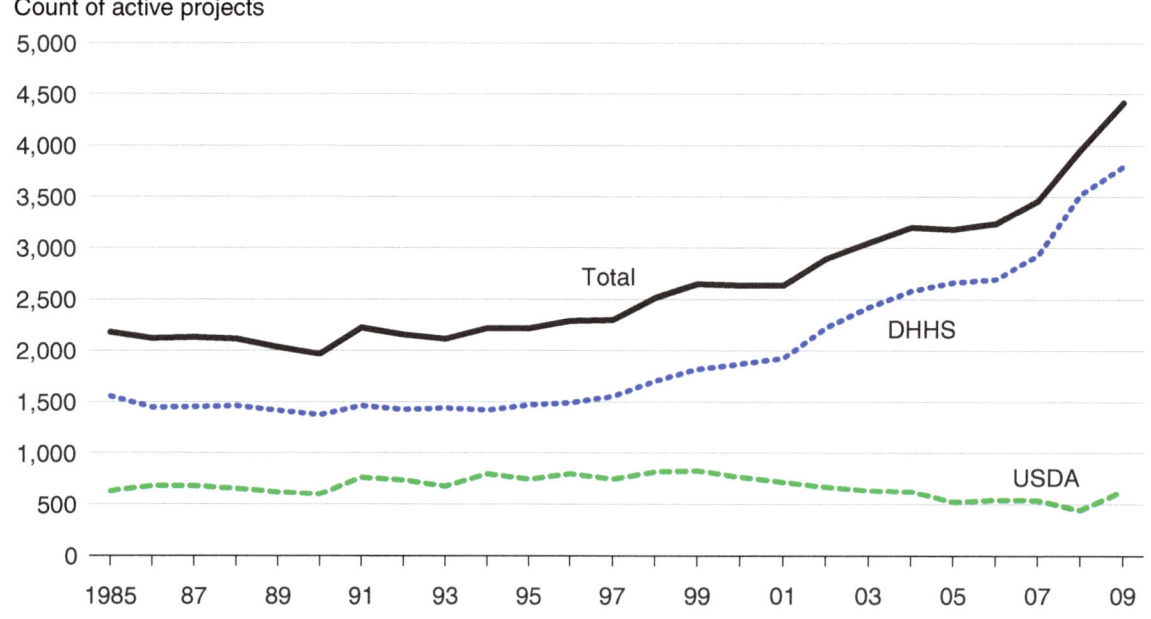

Source: USDA, Economic Research Service based on Human Nutrition Research Information Management data.

As the balance of Federal support shifted toward the DHHS, the mechanisms used to administer Federal support also changed. Federal support mechanisms—the channels through which Federal agencies try to stimulate and advance human nutrition research—have a direct influence on the success of research activities and the accumulation of new knowledge. These mechanisms significantly influence the topics studied, the selection processes determining who gets support, the type of research activities (i.e., laboratory, clinical, social, etc.), and how research findings are communicated and used.

The first major distinction within the structure of Federal support is between intramural and extramural research. Intramural research consists of projects initiated and performed by researchers employed by the Federal Government, typically within Government-owned facilities. Maintaining an intramural research program provides the Federal Government with the capacity to anticipate and respond to public needs in a timely and directed fashion. It is often described as using the unique position of a Federal agency to initiate collaborative and translational research intended to facilitate the movement of research findings into practice (http://irp.nih.gov/about-us/what-is-the-irp).[9] Within DHHS, the NIH performs most nutrition-related intramural research on its main campus in Bethesda, Maryland. The nutrition topics investigated are determined by the various NIH Institutes and Centers. In 2009, The National Institute of Diabetes and Digestive and Kidney Diseases performed the largest share of nutrition-related intramural research, with 33 percent of the active projects. In contrast, the bulk of USDA's intramural nutrition-related research is supported through the Human Nutrition Research Center Program, which maintains a geographically dispersed network of six nutrition research centers located near research universities. These centers performed over 94 percent of all USDA nutrition-related intramural projects in 2009.

The largest and most diverse category of Federal support, extramural research, is performed by non-Federal organizations using Federal funding. Non-Federal organizations include State governments, universities, colleges, research institutes, hospitals, and private companies. Federal extramural support is obtained by these organizations through either "formula" or "non-formula" mechanisms. Formula mechanisms use algorithms defined in the statutes authorizing formula-based Federal programs. For instance, according to the Hatch Act of 1887 (as amended by Public Law 107-293 in 2002), 52 percent of total authorized funds that go to State agricultural experiment stations are distributed in proportion to the State's share of U.S. rural and farm populations. For nutrition research, the USDA is the only agency that administers Federal programs requiring a formula allocation method.

With non-formula funding mechanisms, Federal agencies have greater discretion over the topics, activities, and budgets associated with research support. For instance, Federal agencies regularly design and disseminate requests for applications (RFAs), which are announcements of research funding opportunities in particular areas of interest. These funds are distributed through contracts, grants, and cooperative agreements. Non-formula funding includes earmarks, agency mission-oriented procurement, as well as competitive (e.g., peer-reviewed) research support.

Maintaining a productive nutrition research system requires understanding how differences between non-formula, formula, and intramural funding mechanisms impact the type of research performed

---

[9]Translational research is a broad category of research activities that are intended to facilitate the application of basic research and thereby improve health and well-being. The National Cancer Institute, Translational Research Working Group, provides a more detailed definition at www.cancer.gov/researchandfunding/trwg/TRWG-definition-and-TR-continuum.

and the rate of scientific discovery. All the mechanisms provide money for research, but the costs and behavioral restrictions they impose on researchers can be quite different. Each mechanism creates incentives that shape the choices and behaviors of researchers. For example, some researchers regard formula funding as predictable and flexible because the statutory rules are stable and the selection of topics is delegated to the researchers' home institution (Huffman and Evenson, 2006). Other researchers favor competitive Federal mechanisms using merit-based, peer-review selection because this system is thought to improve the quality of supported research (PCAST 2012).

A growing academic literature is focused on understanding how research incentives influence the selection of topics, knowledge discovery and dissemination, commercial orientation, and research innovation (Aghion et al., 2005; Azoulay et al., 2011; Dasgupta and David, 1994; Gans and Murray, 2012; Manso, 2011). Some of the incentive design characteristics for promoting innovation and creativity identified in this literature include an emphasis on long-term outcomes with a high tolerance for initial failure, low researcher-time costs for preparing research proposals, few restrictions on how findings are communicated, and flexibility to pursue unanticipated lines of inquiry as research progresses.

From 1985 through 2009, project support through non-formula extramural mechanisms grew by 17 percentage points from 69 to 86 percent (fig. 4). This is the dominant form of support used by DHHS. In the same period, formula-based extramural projects declined from 20 to 8 percent of active projects, and intramural projects fell from 11 to 6 percent. The trends reflect the emergence of DHHS as the principal Federal agency supporting nutrition research, as well as administrative decisions to increase the proportion of non-formula support, particularly competitive grants at USDA. However, the implications of these changes for the nutrition research system are unknown. Collection of new data that link Federal mechanisms to research outcomes would be needed before the effects of these changes on knowledge discovery and dissemination could be assessed.

Figure 4
Federal support by type of funding mechanism, 1985-2009

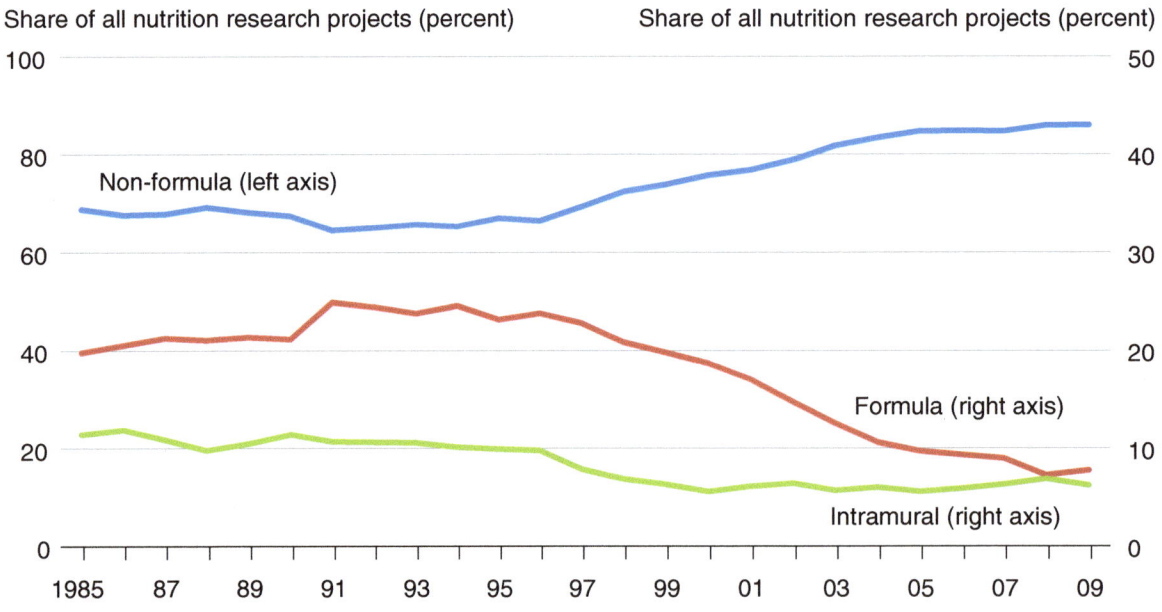

Source: USDA, Economic Research Service based on Human Nutrition Research Information Management data.

Federal Portfolio of Nutrition Research Areas and Research Performers

From 1985 to 2009, agency budget appropriations largely explained the aggregate trends in Federal support for human nutrition research. These aggregate trends altered the structure of Federal support by changing the funding balance among Federal agencies. To the extent that USDA and DHHS have different missions, use different research funding mechanisms, and support different performers within the nutrition research system, these and other influences may have shifted the distribution of Federal support between nutrition research topics and between the organizations that perform the research.

Defining Portfolio Shares Using HNRIM

The Human Nutrition Research Information Management (HNRIM) data system identifies the nature of the nutrition research conducted within each project. Federal agencies reporting to the system assign 1 or more of 37 nutrition subfield (here, topic area) codes to each project.[10] Using these topic area codes, we defined the portfolio of Federal support as shares (in percentage form) distributed across each nutrition topic in the HNRIM classification scheme. Some projects naturally address multiple topics. For example, in 2004 the USDA supported a project titled "obesity prevention for preschool children." This project was assigned to three topic areas: *infant/child nutrition, obesity/anorexia/appetite control*, and *other research in nutrition education*. By assigning individual projects to multiple topic area codes, the HNRIM system captures the practical reality that projects are often relevant to more than one topic area in nutrition research. To construct the portfolio of shares, we parse each project that is assigned to multiple topic areas into the individual components.

We calculated the percentage of projects relevant to each topic by dividing the number of projects assigned to that topic by the total number of project assignments across all 37 topic area codes. Dividing by the total number of assignments from all active projects normalizes the project counts by the level of support. In other words, these shares reflect the distribution of Federal support to each of the 37 nutrition topic areas within a portfolio of fixed size.

Grouping research projects by 37 distinct codes is encyclopedic but cumbersome to present. Distinctions among some codes may be too fine and too numerous for an overview of nutrition support. Fortunately, the HNRIM system provides a means of organizing the codes into six broader research categories:

1. Research on Normal Nutritional Requirements Throughout the Life Cycle
   The lifecycle research area includes all projects that have some relevance to the study and understanding of how normal human nutritional needs change for people in different stages of life. This area contains five topic areas: maternal nutrition, infant/child nutrition (0-12 years), adolescent nutrition (13-18 years), adult nutrition (19-65 years), and nutrition of the elderly (65+ years).

---

[10]In 1980, the Joint Subcommittee on Human Nutrition Research developed a 34-code classification system for human nutrition research that was expanded to 35 codes in 1985. Two codes were added in 1999 for research relevant to nutrition supplements, and the HNRIM database also includes 6 codes for areas of special interest to the NIH. Our analysis is based on the 37-code system used by both USDA and DHHS (ICHNR, 1996).

15

Improving Health Through Nutrition Research: An Overview of the U.S. Nutrition Research System, ERR-182
Economic Research Service/USDA

<u>Selected project title examples:</u>

- Calcium and Phosphorus Nutrition in High-Risk Infants
- Relation Between Nutritional State and Aging.

2. *Research on the Role of Nutrition in Disease, Injury, and Conditions*
   The disease and conditions area contains all projects that have some relevance to the prevention, amelioration, or treatment of diseases, injuries, infections, or conditions. Medical conditions include all projects that have some relevance for understanding the role of nutrition in genetics, function, and the treatment of conditions such as obesity or anorexia. This area contains 11 topic areas of nutrition research: cardiovascular disease; cancer; trauma; infection and immunology; parenteral/enteral/elemental nutrition; other diseases (e.g., osteoporosis, diabetes); obesity/anorexia/appetite control; genetics and nutrition; nutrition and function; nutrient interactions; and other conditions.

   <u>Selected project title examples:</u>

   - Modulation of Xenobiotic Toxicity by Diet
   - Acetylation and N-Oxidation and Colorectal Cancer.

3. *Research on Nutrient Metabolism and Metabolic Mechanisms*
   The metabolism and metabolic mechanisms area contains all projects that examine certain nutrient variables as well as those projects examining nutrient mechanisms and metabolism not related to research in the areas of life cycle, diseases/injury, and medical conditions given above. This area contains nine topic areas: carbohydrates, lipids, alcohols, proteins/amino acids, vitamins, minerals/essential trace elements, water/electrolytes, fiber, and other nutrients in food.

   <u>Selected project title examples:</u>

   - Regulation of Albumin Synthesis by Amino Acids
   - Physico-Chemical Properties of Carbohydrates in Dairy Foods.

4. *Research in Food Sciences*
   The food sciences research area contains all projects within the various disciplines of food science that have a nutritional component. This area contains four topic areas: food composition R&D, bioavailability of nutrients, effects of technology on foods and diets, and other research in food sciences.

   <u>Selected project title examples:</u>

   - Improving Physical Properties of Food Proteins by Chemical Modification
   - Use of Infrared Heat Processing and Its Impact on Food Quality.

5. *Research on Nutrition Monitoring, Education, and Policy*
   The monitoring, education, and policy area contains all projects that have some relevance to the dietary practices and behaviors of human populations. This area contains six topic areas: nutritional status R&D, food consumption survey R&D, studies of methods for informing and educating the public, other research in nutrition education, studies of dietary practices/consumption patterns, and the effects of government policy and socioeconomic factors.

   <u>Selected project title examples:</u>

   - Economic and Behavioral Factors Associated With Food Supplement Usage
   - Food Choice Behavior at Point of Purchase: Assessment and Intervention

16

Improving Health Through Nutrition Research: An Overview of the U.S. Nutrition Research System, ERR-182
Economic Research Service/USDA

6. *Research on Dietary Supplements*

The dietary supplements area contains two topic areas that were added to the HNRIM system in 1999. This area covers all projects that have some relevance for understanding the composition and function of dietary supplements in human nutrition. The two topic areas are: nutrient ingredients of dietary supplements, and botanical and other non-nutrient ingredients in dietary supplements.

Selected project title examples:

- Vitamin B-6 Supplementation and Immune Function
- Multi-vitamins, HAART (highly active antiretroviral therapy) and HIV/AIDS in Uganda.

Distribution of Federal Support Across Major Nutrition Research Areas Is Relatively Stable

Figure 5 displays the Federal portfolio in percentage shares across the six major nutrition research areas for 1985 and 2009. While nearly a quarter of a century separates these two points in time, the distributions across research areas are quite similar. The *Disease, Injury, and Conditions* and *Metabolism and Metabolic Mechanisms* research areas stand out and together constitute 68 and 69 percent of the Federal support in 1985 and 2009, respectively. The stability in these combined shares, however, masks some significant reallocations across the areas. The *Disease, Injury, and Conditions* area grew in portfolio share from 40 percent in 1985 to 49 percent in 2009, while the *Metabolism and Metabolic Mechanisms* area dropped from 28 to 20 percent. The other research area that experienced a significant change in Federal support is *Food Sciences*. The Federal share of active projects in this area declined from 10 to 4 percent. Comparing portfolio shares tells us about how the allocation of support changed over time, but does not account for the overall level of Federal support. In 2009, the Federal Government supported over twice as many active projects as in 1985.

Figure 5
Federal nutrition research portfolio: project distributions in 1985 and 2009

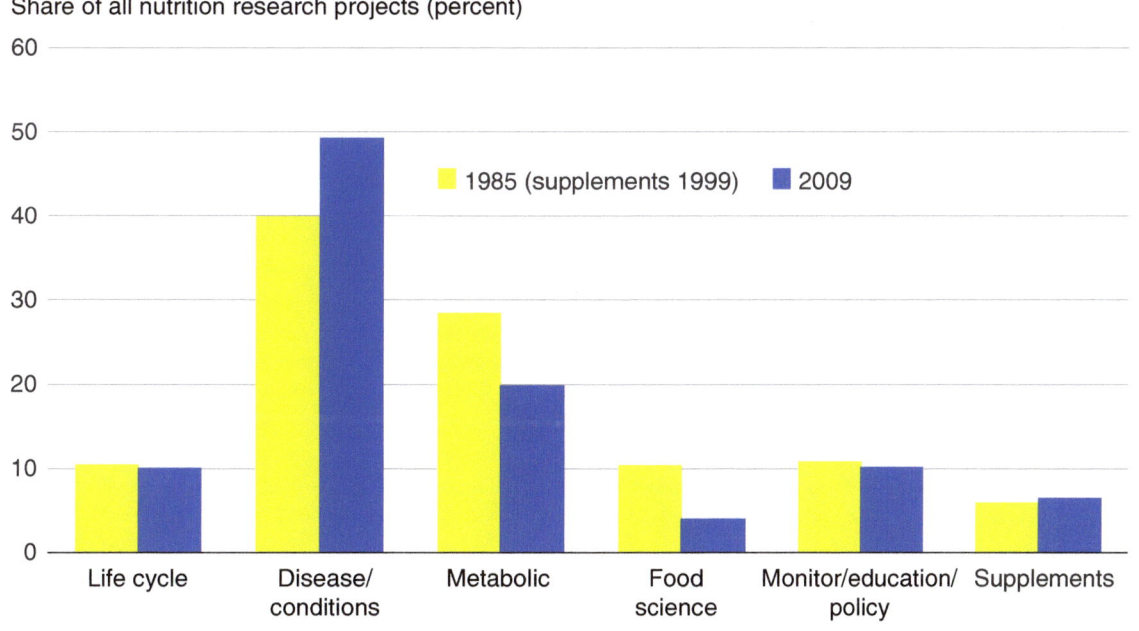

Share of all nutrition research projects (percent)

Source: USDA, Economic Research Service based on Human Nutrition Research Information Management data.

Improving Health Through Nutrition Research: An Overview of the U.S. Nutrition Research System, ERR-182
Economic Research Service/USDA

For the *Metabolism and Metabolic Mechanisms* research area, the number of projects supported increased even though the share in the portfolio declined. For *Food Sciences,* both the number and share declined.

Share of Support for *Disease, Injury,* and *Conditions* Research Increased Due to the *Obesity, Genetics,* and *Other Diseases* Topic Areas

Only 3 of the 11 topic areas composing the *Disease, Injury, and Conditions* research area accounted for most of the growth between 1985 and 2009. The *Obesity/Anorexia/Appetite Control* topic area grew fastest, rising from 3.6 percent to 13.1 percent of the Federal portfolio by 2009 (fig. 6). This topic was the fastest growing within the individual portfolios of both DHHS and USDA. In the DHHS portfolio, the share of active projects related to *Obesity/Anorexia/Appetite Control* increased from 4 percent to 15 percent while the share increased from 1 percent to 7 percent in the USDA nutrition portfolio. The *Genetics* and *Other Diseases* topic areas also grew over this period.[11] The share of active projects related to *Genetics* increased from 3 to 5 percent of the Federal portfolio, while the share related to *Other Diseases* grew from 5 to 9 percent.

Based on the HNRIM data, these increases were not due to changes in the availability of funding through the Federal non-formula, formula, and intramural mechanisms.[12] Instead, program admin-

Figure 6
Trends in Federal nutrition research portfolio shares for obesity, genetics, and other diseases, 1985-2009

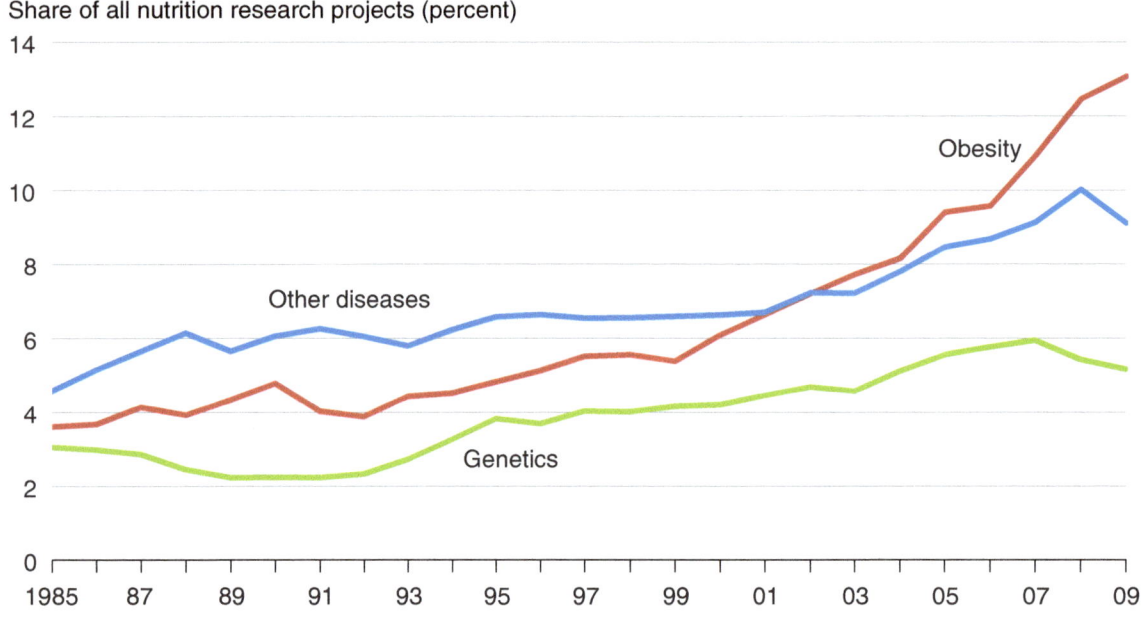

Share of all nutrition research projects (percent)

Source: USDA, Economic Research Service based on Human Nutrition Research Information Management data.

---

[11]The *Other Diseases* topic area includes nutrition research for all diseases except those related to cardiovascular and cancer. For instance, this topic area includes diseases related to eyes, liver, kidney, lung, renal, and mental health.

[12]The Federal share for these topics increased across all the funding mechanisms despite the budget reductions for formula and intramural support. This fact rules out funding availability as the driving reason for the observed increases.

istrators or nutrition researchers determined these trends as a response to influences, such as scientific research opportunities and public needs.

Share of Support for *Metabolism and Metabolic Mechanisms* Research Decreased Due to the *Vitamins, Minerals, and Proteins* Topic Areas

Seven out of the nine topic areas that make up the *Metabolism and Metabolic Mechanisms* research area showed declining shares between 1985 and 2009, with *Vitamins, Minerals*, and *Proteins* leading the decline (fig. 7). Between 1998 and 2009, the Federal portfolio share related to *Vitamins* research dropped 2.6 percentage points, from 6.3 to 3.7 percent. *Minerals* and *Proteins* research experienced similar declines. Once again, based on HNRIM data, these decreases were not due to changes in funding availability through the mix of support mechanisms, but they reflect the decisions by program administrators or nutrition researchers.[13]

Share of Support for *Food Sciences* Decreased Due to the *Food Composition and Effects of Technology on Foods and Diets* Topic Areas

USDA provides almost all Federal support for nutrition research in the *Food Sciences* area, supporting 80 percent of active projects (on average) from 1985 to 2009. Due to this, USDA support largely determines the overall Federal trend. While the Federal shares for each of the four topic

Figure 7

Trends in Federal nutrition research portfolio shares for vitamins, minerals, and proteins, 1985-2009

Share of all nutrition research projects (percent)

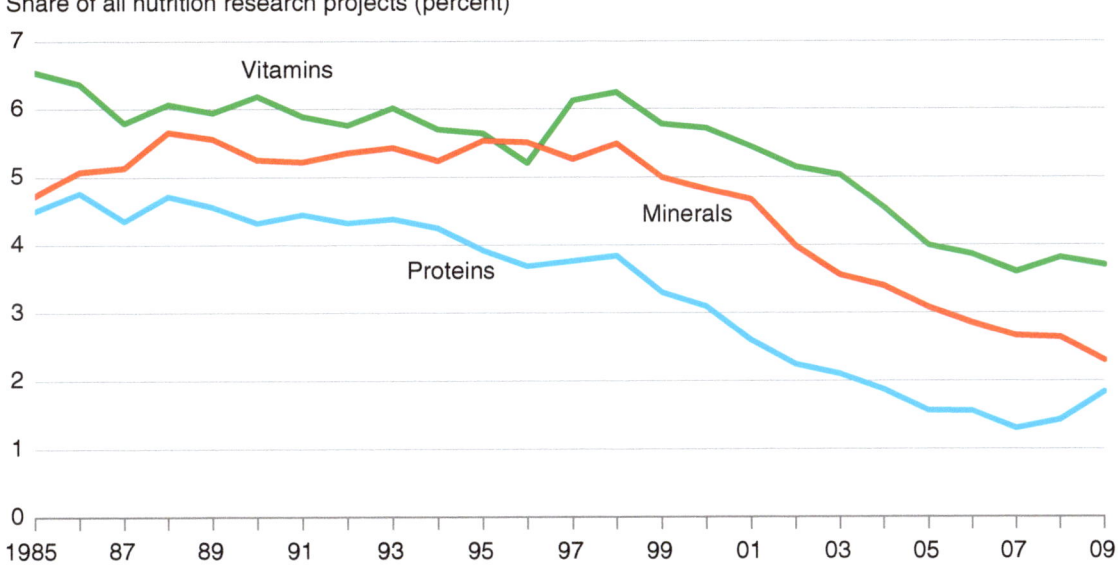

Source: USDA, Economic Research Service based on Human Nutrition Research Information Management data.

---

[13]The Federal share for these topics decreased across all the funding mechanisms despite the budget increases for non-formula support. This fact rules out funding availability as the driving reason for the observed decreases. We investigated the possibility that the introduction of the dietary supplements research area may have caused a reclassification of projects related to vitamins, minerals, and proteins that accelerated the decline in this topic area after 1999. The data do not suggest reclassification is the main driver, but it may have contributed.

Improving Health Through Nutrition Research: An Overview of the U.S. Nutrition Research System, ERR-182
Economic Research Service/USDA

areas within the *Food Sciences* fell, the topics leading the decline were the *Food Composition* and the *Effects of Technology on Foods and Diets*. The Federal share of nutrition research funding going to *Food Composition* research declined steadily from 3.2 percent in 1985 to less than 0.7 percent by 2009 (fig. 8). The Federal share going to research on the *Effects of Technology on Food and Diets* declined from 3.3 percent to 1.2 percent. An increase in the early 1990s seems to reflect the establishment of at least one new food science and nutrition research center by the USDA as authorized in the Food, Agriculture, Conservation, and Trade Act of 1990.

The Portfolio of Federally Supported Organizations That Perform Nutrition Research

Federally supported nutrition research is undertaken by a variety of different organizations. These performing institutions include Federal and State governments, universities and colleges, private companies, medical schools, hospitals, research organizations, and foundations. The distribution of Federal support across these organizations not only reflects the location of skilled research personnel, but also reflects other legal and institutional factors. For instance, the USDA has a unique Federal-State research partnership dating back to the creation of land-grant colleges through the Morrill Act of 1862 and the initiation of formula-based funding for these institutions first authorized by the Hatch Act of 1887. In this partnership, certain universities and colleges are designated by their State legislatures or Congress as cooperating "land-grant" institutions and receive funds on the basis of statutory formulas. Every U.S. State and territory, as well as the District of Columbia, has at least one land-grant institution (APLU, 2012). In addition to these legally based reasons to receive Federal support, performing institutions must also have organizational missions that are consistent with those of the particular Federal agency that provides the funds. So, for instance, nutrition research conducted by medical schools and hospitals is predominantly supported by DHHS and not by USDA.

Figure 8

Trends in Federal nutrition research portfolio shares for food composition and technology, 1985-2009

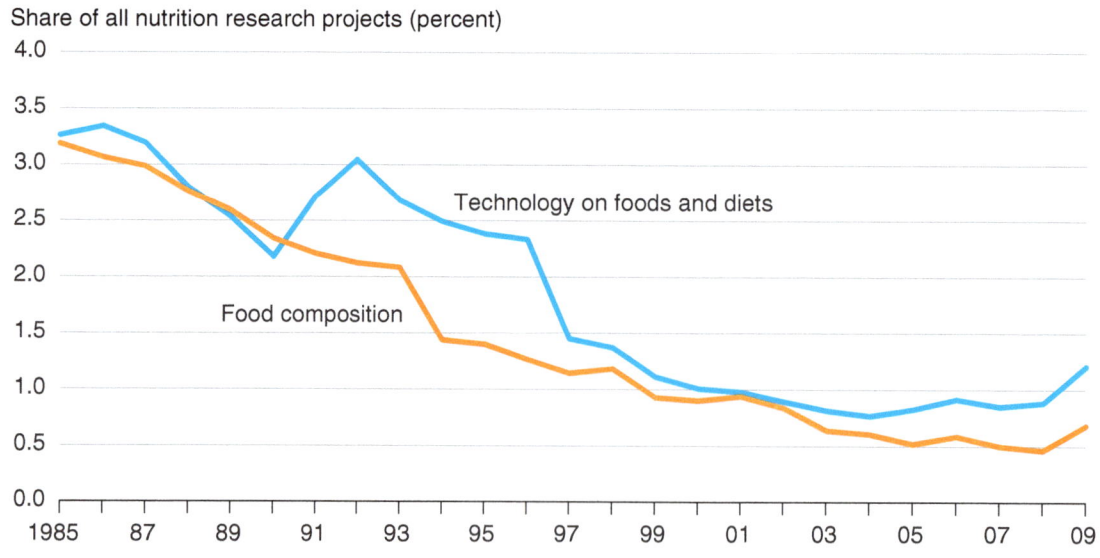

Source: USDA, Economic Research Service based on Human Nutrition Research Information Management data.

Improving Health Through Nutrition Research: An Overview of the U.S. Nutrition Research System, ERR-182
Economic Research Service/USDA

To examine the organizations performing federally supported nutrition research, we classified each organization into one of five groups. The first group, *Government*, includes researchers who work for governmental agencies and consists mostly of research performed in DHHS and USDA facilities supported through intramural funding, but also includes a few State agencies. The second category includes *land-grant universities and colleges* that receive formula funding from the USDA. The data show that nutrition support was widely distributed among these schools. Almost all 1890 land-grant institutions, which are historically Black universities that were established as land-grant institutions under the Second Morrill Act of 1890, received some nutrition support from 1985 to 2009. The third group consists of *non-land-grant universities and colleges*. These research institutions do not receive formula funding from the USDA. Private *companies* that receive Federal support for nutrition research comprise group four. The final group, *Other*, is mostly medical schools and hospitals, but also includes not-for-profit research institutes, foundations, and associations.

Figure 9 illustrates how the portfolio of federally supported organizations that perform nutrition research changed over the 25-year period covered by the HNRIM database. For each group of organizations, two columns are presented. The first column shows the percentage of nutrition projects performed by that group in 1985, and the second column shows the percentage for 2009.[14] The share of Federal nutrition research projects performed by government researchers fell from 12 percent in 1985 to 6 percent in 2009. Land-grant universities are also performing a smaller share of federally supported nutrition projects, a drop of 12 percentage points from 34 percent in 1985 to 22 percent in 2009. The share of federally supported nutrition research performed by the other three groups increased over the 25-year period. Non-land-grant universities and colleges show an increase of 11 percentage points to reach 41 percent of total nutrition projects in 2009. The *Other* category of institutions also increased from 22 percent to 29 percent of all active federally supported nutrition projects. Private companies performed only a small share of projects in both 1985 and 2009.

Figure 9

Federally supported nutrition research projects by institution type, 1985 and 2009

Percent of all nutrition research projects

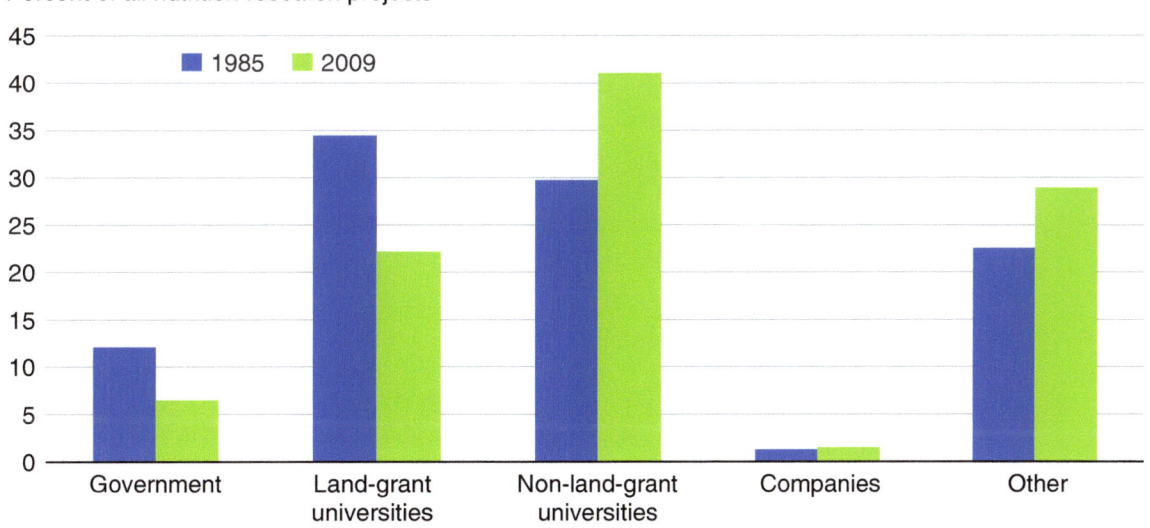

Source: USDA, Economic Research Service based on Human Nutrition Research Information Management data.

---

[14]Due to the large number of performing institutions that required manual searches to determine the proper classification, we only analyzed organizations active in 1985 and 2009.

Improving Health Through Nutrition Research: An Overview of the U.S. Nutrition Research System, ERR-182
Economic Research Service/USDA

Conclusion

The U.S. nutrition research system is a vital component of the larger communication network linking nutritional content to dietary choices and health outcomes. It provides the knowledge foundation that fuels continued progress toward better health. Understanding the structure and function of the U.S. nutrition research system, along with the development of diagnostic indicators, can help identify current and emerging issues, such as the impacts of alternative funding mechanisms and policies on research incentives and performance, and research gaps or opportunities requiring further scientific inquiry.

This report takes a first step in that direction, identifying the range of organizations that sponsor nutrition research in the United States and documenting the availability of data on R&D investments. Generally, publicly available data are limited except for Federal investments. The Human Nutrition Research Information Management (HNRIM) database documents the R&D investments by the main Federal agencies supporting nutrition research, DHHS and USDA. The HNRIM data allow us to analyze the level and trends in Federal support across agencies, between topics within the field of nutrition research, and among performing institutions. A number of broad observations emerge that may help inform future studies on the vitality and efficiency of the U.S. nutrition research system. These are:

- Measuring and tracking Federal support for nutrition research would improve if the HNRIM database expanded to other Federal agencies and offered greater standardization. For instance, renewed participation by Federal agencies such as the National Science Foundation and the U.S. Department of Defense would significantly enhance Federal coverage. Standardization across agencies of the processes for identifying nutrition projects, coding the project's nutrition fields, and parsing the share of a project's resources devoted to nutrition would be valuable, especially as new computer-based categorization algorithms like the NIH Research Condition and Disease Classification system are implemented.

- Based on the HNRIM database, this report identifies major shifts in the underlying funding mechanisms used by Federal agencies to support nutrition research. Each of the mechanisms—formula, non-formula, and intramural—use different project selection criteria and impose different costs on individual researchers. Future research examining how alternative Federal mechanisms influence choice of research topic, results, and productivity could guide policy formulation.

- As HNRIM has lost coverage of Federal agencies that support nutrition research, its future utility in helping answer questions about the size and direction of Federal support for nutrition is limited. New initiatives that collect data on private-sector investments in nutrition research would provide useful information.

- The knowledge produced by the U.S. nutrition research system is vital. The volume of knowledge produced and the channels through which this knowledge flows are not well documented. Various commercial databases such as Elsevier's Scopus or Thomson-Reuters Web of Science offer extensive information on professional journal publications that may be used to construct indicators of knowledge output based on publications and knowledge flows based on citation analysis. The patent and trademark data at the U.S. Patent and Trademark Office could also be used to assess nutrition innovation and the commercialization of products and services.

22

Improving Health Through Nutrition Research: An Overview of the U.S. Nutrition Research System, ERR-182
Economic Research Service/USDA

References

Aghion, P., M. Dewatripont, and J.C. Stein. 2005. "Acacemic freedom, private-sector focus, and the process of innovation." National Bureau of Economic Research Working Paper No. 11542, Aug.

American Dietetic Association (ADA). 2009. "Position of the American Dietetic Association: Functional Foods," *Journal of the American Dietetic Association* 109(4): 735-746.

Arrow, K. 1962. "Economic Welfare and the Allocation of Resources for Invention," *The Rate and Direction of Inventive Activity* (R.R. Nelson, ed.) Princeton, NJ: Princeton University Press.

Association of Public and Land-grant Universities (APLU). 2012. "The Land-Grant Tradition," http://www.aplu.org/document.doc?id=780.

Azoulay, P., J.S. Graff Zivin, and G. Manso. 2011. "Incentives and creativity: evidence from the academic life sciences," *RAND Journal of Economics* 42(3): 527-554.

Branscomb, L.M., and R. Florida. 1998. "Challenges to Technology Policy in a Changing Economy," *Investing in Innovation* (L.M. Branscomb and J.H. Keller, eds.) Cambridge, MA: MIT Press.

Centers for Disease Control and Prevention (CDC). 2014. "Childhood Obesity Facts" updated Feb. 27, 2014, http://www.cdc.gov/healthyyouth/obesity/facts.htm

Centers for Disease Control and Prevention (CDC). 2004. "Spina Bifida and Anencephaly Before and After Folic Acid Mandate—United States, 1995-1996 and 1999-2000," *Morbidity and Mortality Weekly Report* 53(17): 362-365, http://www.cdc.gov/mmwr/preview/mmwrhtml/mm5317a3.htm.

Cinnamon, B. 2009. "Results from the Functional Foods and Natural Health Products Survey – 2007." Statistics Canada, Business Special Surveys and Technology Statistics Division.

Dasgupta, P., and P.A. David. 1994. "Toward a new economics of science," *Research Policy* 23(5): 487-521.

Davis, C., and E. Saltos. 1999. "Dietary Recommendations and How They Have Changed Over Time." *America's Eating Habits: Changes and Consequences.* U.S. Department of Agriculture, Economic Research Service, AIB-750. http://www.ers.usda.gov/publications/aib750/aib750.pdf.

Demonty, I., R.T. Ras, H.C.M. van der Knaap, G.S.M.J.E. Duchateau, L. Meijer, P.L. Zock, J.M. Geleijnse, and E.A. Trautwein. 2009. "Continuous Dose-Response Relationship of the LDL-Cholesterol–Lowering Effect of Phytosterol Intake," *The Journal of Nutrition*, 193(2): 271-284.

Finkelstein, Eric. A., Justin G. Trogden, Joel W. Cohen, and William Dietz. 2009. "Annual Medical Spending Attributable to Obesity: Payer and Service-specific Estimates," *Health Affairs* 28(5): w822-w831.

Fuglie, K.O., P.W. Heisey, J.L. King, C.E. Pray, K. Day-Rubenstein, D. Schimmelpfennig, S.L. Wang, and R. Karmarkar-Deshmukh. 2011. *Research Investments and Market Structure in the Food Processing, Agricultural Input, and Biofuel Industries Worldwide.* U.S. Department of Agriculture, Economic Research Service, ERR-130. Dec.

23

Improving Health Through Nutrition Research: An Overview of the U.S. Nutrition Research System, ERR-182
Economic Research Service/USDA

Gans, J., and F. Murray. 2012. "Funding scientific knowledge: Selection, disclosure and the public-private portfolio," *The Rate and Direction of Inventive Activity: A New Agenda*, Chicago, IL: University of Chicago Press.

General Accounting Office (GAO). 1982. "Progress made in Federal human nutrition research planning and coordination; some improvements needed."

Guenther, P.M., W.Y. Juan, M. Lino, H. Hiza, T. Fungwe, and R. Lucas. 2008. "Diet Quality of Low-Income and Higher Income Americans in 2003-2004 as Measured by the Healthy Eating Index-2005," *Nutrition Insight* 42. U.S. Department of Agriculture, Center for Nutrition Policy and Promotion.

Harvard School of Public Health. 2014. "Genes are not destiny." http://www.hsph.harvard.edu/obesity-prevention-source/obesity-causes/genes-and-obesity/#references.

Huffman, W.E., and R.E. Evenson. 2006. "Do formula or competitive grant funds have greater impacts on state agricultural productivity?" *American Journal of Agricultural Economics* 88(4): 783-798.

Interagency Committee on Human Nutrition Research (ICNHR). 1996. "The Human Nutrition Research and Information Management System Definition of Human Nutrition Research: Fifteenth Progress Report." http://hnrim.nih.gov/yearlyreports.aspx.

International Food and Information Council (IFIC). 2013. "Functional Foods Consumer Survey, Executive Research Report." http://www.foodinsight.org/Home.aspx.

Institute of Food Technologists (IFT). 2005. "Functional Foods: Opportunities and Challenges." Institute of Food Technologists Expert Report, http://www.ift.org/Knowledge-Center/Read-IFT-Publications/Science-Reports/Scientific-Status-Summaries/Functional-Foods.aspx.

Institute of Medicine (IOM). 2013. "Nutrition education in the K-12 curriculum: The role of national standards: Workshop summary," Washington, DC: The National Academies Press, 2013.

Institute of Medicine. 2005. "Dietary Reference Intakes for Energy, Fat, Fatty Acids, Cholesterol, Protein, and Amino Acids (Macronutrients): A Report of the Panel on Macronutrients, Subcommittees on Upper Reference Levels of Nutrients and Interpretation and Uses of Dietary Reference Intakes, and the Standing Committee on the Scientific Evaluation of Dietary Reference Intakes." Washington, DC: National Academy of Sciences Press.

Institute of Medicine. 1998. "Scientific opportunities and public needs: Improving priority setting and public input at the National Institutes of Health," Washington, DC: National Academy of Sciences Press, 1998.

Institute of Medicine. 1994. *Opportunities in the nutrition and Food Sciences: Research Challenges and the Next Generation of Investigators*, Washington, DC: National Academy of Sciences Press.

Manso, G. 2011. "Motivating Innovation," *Journal of Finance* 165(5): 1823-1859.

Martinez, Steve W. 2013. *Introduction of New Food Products With Voluntary Health- and Nutrition-Related Claims, 1989-2010,* EIB-108, U.S. Department of Agriculture, Economic Research Service, Feb.

24

Improving Health Through Nutrition Research: An Overview of the U.S. Nutrition Research System, ERR-182
Economic Research Service/USDA

Murphy, K.M., and R.H. Topel. 2006. "The Value of Health and Longevity," *Journal of Political Economy* 114(5): 871-904

National Research Council (NRC). 2003. "Frontiers in agricultural research: Food, health, environments, and communities," Washington, DC: National Academies of Sciences Press.

National Science Foundation, National Center for Science and Engineering Statistics. 2013. Survey of Research and Development at Universities and Colleges, Integrated Science and Engineering Resources Data System (WebCASPAR) (https://webcaspar.nsf.gov).

Nelson, R.R. 1959. The Simple Economics of Basic Scientific Research," *Journal of Political Economy* 67:297-306.

Ohlhorst, S., R. Russell, D. Bier, D.M. Klurfeld, Z. Li, J.R. Mein, J. Milner, A.C. Ross, P. Stover, and E. Konopka. 2013. "Nutrition Research to Affect Food and a Healthy Life Span," *American Journal of Clinical Nutrition* 98(2): 620-625.

President's Council of Advisors on Science and Technology (PCAST). 2012. *Report to the President on Agricultural Preparedness and the Agricultural Research Enterprise*, Executive office of the President, December 2012.

Price Waterhouse Coopers. 2009. "Leveraging growth in the emerging functional foods industry: Trends and market opportunities."

Rahkovsky, I., S. Martinez, and F. Kuchler. 2012. *New Food Choices Free of Trans Fats Better Align U.S. Diets with Health Recommendations*. EIB-95, U.S. Dept. of Agriculture, Economic Research Service, April.

Rosenberg, I. H. 2009. "History of the USDA Human Nutrition Research Center on Aging at Tufts University," *The Journal of Nutrition* 139: 192-193.

Ribaudo, M., F. Kuchler, and L. Mancino. 2008. "Market Failures: When the Invisible Hand Gets Shaky," *Amber Waves*, U.S. Dept. of Agriculture, Economic Research Service. Nov.

Schimmelpfennig, D., and P. Heisey. 2009. *U.S. Public Agricultural Research: Changes in Funding Sources and Shifts in Emphasis, 1980-2005*. EIB-45, U.S. Dept. of Agriculture, Economic Research Service, March.

University College London. 2013. "How 'obesity gene' triggers weight gain." http://www.ucl.ac.uk/news/news-articles/0713/15072013-How-obesity-gene-triggers-weight-gain-Batterham.

U.S. Department of Agriculture, Food and Nutrition Service (FNS). 2013. Website for Healthy, Hunger-Free Kids Act of 2010, http://www.fns.usda.gov/cnd/Governance/Legislation/CNR_2010.htm.

U.S. Department of Health and Human Services, Food and Drug Administration. 2013. "Tentative Determination Regarding Partially Hydrogenated Oils; Request for Comments and for Scientific Data and Information: A Notice by the Food and Drug Administration on 11/08/2013. *Federal Register* Vol. 78, No. 217: 67169-67175. http://www.gpo.gov/fdsys/pkg/FR-2013-11-08/pdf/2013-26854.pdf.

Viscusi, W.K., and J.E. Aldy. 2003. "The value of a statistical life: A critical review of market estimates throughout the world," *The Journal of Risk and Uncertainty* 27(1): 5-76.

Appendix—The Relationship Between Project Counts and Project Awards

Support for nutrition research can be characterized by the number of projects for which the Federal Government provided funding or by the funding itself. If all projects were funded alike—awarded the same dollar amount—it would not make any difference whether support was characterized by number of projects or by dollars. However, when the average financial award per project changes over time, trend analyses using the two approaches will yield different magnitudes, particularly when calculating growth rates.

At the beginning of this study, no project-level financial award amounts were available in HNRIM. In an effort to check the validity of using project counts, the authors evaluated other publicly available databases at the National Institutes of Health (NIH) as potential sources of project-level financial data. The NIH "Awards by Location" Web search page (http://report.nih.gov/award/index.cfm) inventories annual extramural grant and contract awards for research and training projects. Beginning in 1992 (the earliest year), annual project-level data were downloaded, cleaned of obvious errors, and appended to form a project-level database containing project IDs and award amounts. A matching program was used to standardize the project identification numbers for these data. A similar program was written for the HNRIM database. Using these programs, an 88-percent match rate was achieved between the two databases, and the financial award amounts were retrieved and appended to the HNRIM project records for those NIH extramural projects.

Subsequently, the project-level award amounts associated with the HNRIM database became available. These data significantly improved our information on project-level financial awards by adding other Federal agencies such as the USDA, as well as intramural funding amounts. By combining these new data to our matched data, we were able to perform a check on the HNRIM financial amounts for NIH extramural projects. This check verified the accuracy of the HNRIM financial data but also showed that some entries reporting $0 financial awards in HNRIM were not "no-cost" extensions, just missing data. Other than DHHS, all Federal agencies that support nutrition research report $0 as the funded amount for a significant number of projects. Among USDA projects, 15 percent report $0 financial awards. For the other 6 agencies, over 63 percent of the project records have $0 as the funding amount (table A1).

Table A1
Financial information for project-year records, 1985-2009 (%)

Financial data greater than $0	Federal agencies			
	DHHS	USDA	OTHER	Total
Yes	70,062 (92%)	18,327 (85%)	1,153 (37%)	89,542 (89%)
No	5,720 (8%)	3,179 (15%)	1,964 (63%)	10,863 (11%)
Total	75,782	21,506	3,117	100,405

Source: USDA, Economic Research Service calculations based on Human Nutrition Research Information Management and National Institutes of Health databases

Consistent results across the project count and expenditure approaches depend on the assumption that the average award amount per project remained relatively constant over time. To check this, we calculated the average dollars per project for DHHS and USDA using the HNRIM data. To do so, we imputed missing financial award data. We separated the project-year records with $0 financial awards into two groups: no-cost extensions and missing data. We defined projects as no-cost extensions when they were part of a multiyear project that had at least 1 year of non-zero award information. For these records, the $0 financial award entries in HNRIM are assumed to be correct. For the remainder, we imputed a financial award amount based on the average for the agency and fiscal year. For example, we used the average award amount for non-missing USDA projects in 2009 to replace any missing award data for projects supported by the USDA in 2009.

For DHHS and USDA, figure A1 presents the trends in average award per project in real dollars.[15] In 1985, an average NIH nutrition project received about $393,000 in annual support. This amount peaked at $504,000 in 2001, then declined to $384,000 by 2009. The peak occurred in the middle of the 1999-2003 period over which the NIH research budget doubled (in nominal terms). With this unusual infusion of funds, project size temporarily increased. Comparing project size in 2009 with 1985, it appears that project size declined at an average annual rate of 0.1 percent, but regression analysis showed no statistically significant linear trend in dollars per project over time. Compared to DHHS, USDA project size was more stable. In 1985, USDA nutrition projects received an average of about $250,000. By 2009, average project size had decreased to $180,000, which represents an average annual decrease of 1.4 percent. Again, regression analysis did not show this decline to be statistically different from zero for the 25-year period.

Figure A1
Average dollars per nutrition research project, 1985-2009

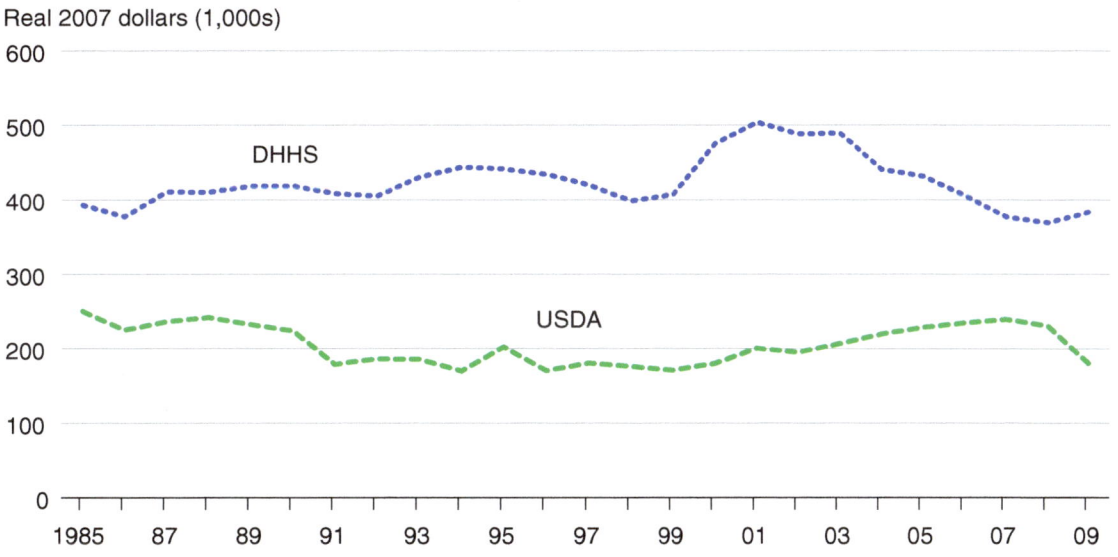

Real 2007 dollars (1,000s)

Source: USDA, Economic Research Service based on Human Nutrition Research Information Management data and the Biomedical Research and Development Price Index.

---

[15]Adjustments for inflation were made using the Biomedical Research and Development Price Index, 2007 reference year. The index is available at http://officeofbudget.od.nih.gov/gbiPriceIndexes.html.